EXPLORE PORTUGAL

"Unveiling Portugal's Charms: A Traveller's Guide to Exquisite Landscapes, Rich Culture, and Memorable Adventures"

ERIKSEN DRAKE

Table of content

Introduction

Welcome to the enamoring excursion of investigating Portugal holiday. Settled on the Iberian Promontory, Portugal is enticed with an embroidery of history, culture, and normal excellence that guarantees a remarkable encounter. As you turn the pages of this aide, plan to be captivated by the thin roads of Lisbon, the riverside appeal of Porto, the sun-kissed seashores of the Algarve, and the fantasy scenes of Sintra. Whether you're a set of experiences buff, a foodie looking for culinary enjoyment, or a globe-trotter looking for open-air capers, Portugal offers a different embroidery of encounters. This guide is your visa to finding the substance of Portugal — its unlikely treasures, rich practices, and warm cordiality. Embrace the appeal of this captivating objective and let your Portuguese experience start!

Welcoming Portugal

As you step onto the sun-doused shores of Portugal, a warm hug of history and culture is standing by. In this segment, we dive into the quintessence of Portugal's inviting soul, making way for your investigation. Find the cadenced beat of life in conventional areas, enjoy the fragrance of newly prepared cakes, and submerge yourself in the immortal customs that characterise this captivating country. From the dynamic city roads to the serene open country, Portugal stretches out a cordial greeting to each explorer, welcoming you to uncover the tales woven into its cobblestone pathways and to turn out to be essential for its rich embroidery. Go along with us as we set out on an excursion through the essence of a country that welcomes you to visit as well as to have a place.

Essential Travel Tips

Plan Ahead: Exploration your objective, grasp nearby traditions, and plan your schedule ahead of time.

Pack Wisely: Pack just basics, actually take a look at the weather conditions figure, and remember significant reports like visas and travel protection.

Stay Connected: Offer your agenda with somebody you trust, and keep significant contacts convenient.

Safety First: Know about your environmental factors, utilise trustworthy transportation, and keep your possessions secure.

Health Precautions: Convey important drugs, remain hydrated, and be mindful of neighbourhood food and water.

Money Matters: Illuminate your bank about your movement dates, convey some neighbourhood money, and have a blend of instalment choices.

Emergency Information: Realise neighbourhood crisis numbers, find the closest government office or department, and have an essential medical aid pack.

Cultural Respect: Regard neighbourhood customs and customs. Become familiar with a couple of fundamental expressions in the nearby language; it goes far.

Tech Essentials: Keep your gadgets charged, utilise secure Wi-Fi, and have reinforcement duplicates of significant reports in a computerised structure.

Adaptability: Things may not go as arranged all the time. Remain adaptable and embrace the surprises for a more pleasant excursion.

Chapter:1

Lisbon

Welcome to Lisbon, a city that flawlessly mixes custom and innovation along the banks of the Tagus Stream. In this energetic capital, investigate the notable regions of Alfama, where the reverberations of Fado music entwined with the city's old soul. Walk around Bairro Alto's enthusiastic roads, decorated with bright road workmanship and bursting at the seams with the buzz of contemporary life.

Submerge yourself in the social extravagance of galleries, for example, the Museu Nacional do Azulejo, observing Portugal's tile-production legacy. Wonder about the notorious Belém Pinnacle and enjoy the pleasantness of pastel de nata by the Jerónimos Cloister. Lisbon's appeal lies in its memorable milestones as well as in the veritable warmth of its kin. As you cross its slopes and valleys, Lisbon welcomes you to embrace its exceptional mix of old-world appeal and current energy.

City of Seven Hills

Lisbon, Portugal's capital, unfurls its story across seven slopes, each offering a novel viewpoint on the city's rich history and energetic present. From the levels of São Jorge Palace, where archaic walls murmur stories of successes, to the energetic roads of Bairro Alto, where contemporary life beats with energy, the seven slopes shape the personality of this enthralling city.

Meander through Alfama's labyrinth-like entryways, where Fado music catches the spirit of Lisbon. Appreciate all-encompassing perspectives from the grand perspectives that dab the scene. These slopes are not simply geological highlights; they are vantage focuses to observe the city's development, from its sea magnificence days in Belém to the cutting-editorial centre points that flourish today. Lisbon, the city of seven slopes, welcomes you to rise its slants and find the different stories carved into its captivating geology.

Historic Alfama

Notable Alfama

In the core of Lisbon, the cobbled roads of Alfama reverberate with stories of hundreds of years past. In this section, meander through the limited rear entryways and find the spirit of the city's most seasoned locale. From the impressive São Jorge Palace, review the red-tiled rooftops and twisted roads that breeze their direction down to the Tagus Waterway.

Investigate notable tourist spots like the Lisbon Church, where the city's set of experiences is carved in stone, and experience the energetic neighbourhood culture in Fado houses, where melancholic songs express the soul of Alfama. Let the fragrance of conventional Portuguese food guide you to stowed-away bars, and don't miss the energetic air of the Feira da Ladra swap meet, where fortunes and stories interlace. Alfama, with its middle age, beguile, and immortal charm welcomes you to step into a living embroidery of Lisbon's rich and various legacy.

Belém and Its Landmarks

Excursion to Belém, a region in Lisbon where history unfurls along the banks of the Tagus Waterway. In this section, we investigate famous milestones that stand as demonstrations of Portugal's Period of Disclosure. Wonder about the loftiness of the Jerónimos Cloister, a show-stopper of Manueline design, and consider the meaning of the Landmark to the Disclosures, which honours the nation's wayfarers.

Enjoy the overwhelming pleasantness of pastel de nata at the prestigious Pastéis de Belém pastry kitchen, a culinary practice that has pleased taste buds for quite a long time. Go for a comfortable walk along the riverfront, where the Belém Pinnacle remains as a sentinel protecting the entry to the city. Belém, with its verifiable loftiness and sea enchantment, welcomes you to submerge yourself in the soul of investigation that formed Portugal's past.

Modern Vibes in Bairro Alto

Present-day Energies in Bairro Alto

Experience the unique beat of contemporary Lisbon in the enthusiastic area of Bairro Alto. In this section, jump into the enthusiastic roads enhanced with dynamic road craftsmanship, where advancement meets with notable appeal. Investigate stylish stores, varied bars, and stylish bistros that line the tight rear entryways, making a dynamic air constantly.

Bairro Alto wakes up into the evening, offering a nightlife scene that ranges from cosy Fado houses to stylish clubs. Feel the mood of Lisbon's cutting-edge music and dance scene as you blend with local people and individual explorers. Amid the memorable structures and conventional façades, Bairro Alto stands as a demonstration of Lisbon's capacity to flawlessly mix its rich past with the throbbing energy of the present. Investigate the cutting-edge energies of Bairro Alto and find a side of Lisbon that is however powerful as it very well might be extraordinary.

Chapter:2

Porto

Welcome to Porto, Portugal's second-biggest city, where the Douro Waterway effortlessly winds its direction through an embroidery of notable appeal and dynamic culture. In this section, investigate the UNESCO-recorded Ribeira locale, where bright houses reflect in the waters, causing a beautiful situation. Meander through limited rear entryways decorated with clothing lines, uncovering the credibility of Porto's routine.

Enjoy a tangible excursion through the port wine basements, where extremely old customs are saved. Wonder about the notorious Dom Luís I Scaffold, associating the clamouring Ribeira with the port wine hotels of Vila Nova de Gaia. Porto, with its rich oceanic history and inviting soul, welcomes you to appreciate its culinary joys, from Francesinha sandwiches to new fish. Whether walking around the riverbanks or rising the slopes for all-encompassing perspectives, Porto coaxes you to find the heart and character of this captivating city.

Riverside Elegance

Experience the captivating appeal of Porto's riverside tastefulness. In this part, we explore the environmental region of Ribeira, where memorable structures enhanced with beautiful exteriors line the banks of the Douro Stream. Meander along the cobblestone roads, where the reverberations of nautical stories resound with each step.

Investigate the beguiling Ribeira Square, a clamouring centre where local people and guests meet to appreciate riverside bistros and absorb the lively environment. Cross the famous Dom Luís I Scaffold, a compositional show-stopper that associates Ribeira with the port wine basements of Vila Nova de Gaia. From relaxed boat rides on the Douro to tasting port wine at dusk, find the riverside polish that characterises Porto and adds a hint of immortal appeal to this charming city.

Exploring the Ribeira District

Set out on an excursion through Porto's spirit in the noteworthy Ribeira region. In this section, wander along restricted cobblestone roads, where extremely old structures grandstand complex tilework and vivid veneers. Feel the heartbeat of the city as you experience vivacious business sectors, customary bars, and the charming hints of road performers.

Visit Ribeira Square, a dynamic social event place by the Douro Stream, where the beat of neighbourhood life converges with the immortal magnificence of the environmental elements. Investigate the archaic Porto House of Prayer and dig into the locale's sea history at the Casa do Infante. Whether tasting coffee at a riverside bistro or taking a boat voyage along the Douro, the Ribeira locale welcomes you to drench yourself in

Porto's rich legacy and experience the certifiable warmth of its kin.

Port Wine Cellars Experience

Port Wine Basements Experience

Enjoy the rich legacy of Porto with an excursion into its popular port wine basements. In this part, find the mysteries of the winemaking system that has characterised the city for a long time. Adventure into the cool, faintly lit basements of Vila Nova de Gaia, where oak barrels house the valuable nectar of the Douro Valley.

Visit notorious wine cabins like Sandeman, Graham's, or alternately Taylor's, each with its exceptional history and mixes. Draw in your faculties with directed tastings, relishing the intricacies of matured brownish and rare ports. Find out about the complex specialty of mixing that creates the particular flavours inseparable from

Porto. The port wine basements offer a tasting experience as well as an excursion through time, uncovering the craftsmanship and customs that make Porto an incredibly famous objective for wine lovers

.

Majestic Bridges of Porto

Superb Extensions of Porto

Wonder about the compositional beauty traversing the Douro Stream as we investigate the lofty scaffolds of Porto. In this part, look at the notable Dom Luís I Extension, a twofold deck iron wonder that interfaces Porto with Vila Nova de Gaia. Stroll across its upper level for all-encompassing perspectives on the city or go for a relaxed walk on the lower deck, feeling the waterway breeze.

Find the Arrábida Scaffold, a link that remains magnificent and adds a cutting-edge touch to Porto's horizon. Cross the exquisite Maria Pia Extension, a demonstration crafted by Gustave

Eiffel, offering a brief look into Porto's modern past. These extensions interface the city as well as stand as images of designing ability and imaginative tastefulness. Go along with us as we navigate these sublime designs, each recounting a one-of-a-kind story of Porto's association with the Douro Stream.

Chapter: 3

The Algarve

Welcome to the sun-kissed heaven of the Algarve, Portugal's southernmost district. In this section, investigate a shore embellished with brilliant sea shores, emotional precipices, and beguiling fishing towns. From the dynamic energy of Faro to the beautiful excellence of Lagos, the Algarve welcomes you to submerge yourself in its assorted scenes and rich social embroidery.

Enjoy the delights of the ocean with water sports, or just loosen up on unblemished seashores like Praia da Marinha. Navigate the shocking bluffs of Ponta da Piedade for amazing all-encompassing perspectives. Find the Algarve's culinary joys, enjoying new fish in shoreline cafés. Whether looking for unwinding or experience, the Algarve offers a sanctuary of regular magnificence and social lavishness that dazzles each voyager.

Sun-Kissed Coastline

Relax in the brilliance of the Algarve's sun-kissed shore. In this section, we investigate the brilliant sea shores that stretch along the sky-blue Atlantic Sea. From the enthusiastic shores of Albufeira to the tranquil magnificence of Praia da Rocha, each ocean side discloses its novel appeal.

Find stowed inlets outlined by limestone precipices, similar to the personal Praia da Marinha. Take part in water exercises in free, welcoming waters, or just loosen up on the warm sands. The Algarve's sun-kissed shore coaxes with a commitment of serenity and regular magnificence, welcoming you to loosen up and ingest the waterfront wizardry that characterises this spellbinding district.

Pristine Beaches

Enjoy the charm of the Algarve's immaculate seashores. In this part, we uncover stretches of shore where brilliant sands meet completely clear waters, making a sanctuary for sunseekers and nature fans the same.

Investigate the untainted excellence of Praia da Marinha, known for its famous limestone precipices and turquoise waters. Feel the delicate sands underneath your feet at Praia da Falésia, where ochre-shaded precipices give a shocking background. Whether it's the energetic energy of Praia de Alvor or the peacefulness of Praia da Ilha Deserta, the Algarve's perfect sea shores guarantee snapshots of serenity and normal magnificence. Go along with us as we set out on an excursion to these beachfront jewels, where the gathering of land and ocean turns into an immortal exhibition.

Charming Coastal Towns

Enchanting Beachfront Towns

Dive into the captivating appeal of the Algarve's enchanting beachfront towns. In this section, we meander through cobblestone roads fixed with whitewashed houses decorated with beautiful accents. Investigate the notable appeal of Lagos, where antiquated city walls share accounts of oceanic undertakings.

Find the fishing town feel of Alvor, where thin back streets lead to beautiful harbours and fish cafés. Feel the casual energies of Carvoeiro, a town settled between sensational bluffs and tranquil sea shores. Each waterfront town in the Algarve has its one-of-a-kind person, offering a mix of history, culture, and ocean-side quietness. Go along with us as we wander through these enchanting safe houses, where time appears to dial back, welcoming you to enjoy the waterfront wizardry of the Algarve.

Seafood Delights

Leave on a culinary excursion along the Algarve's shoreline, where fish delights become the overwhelming focus. In this section, appreciate the kinds of the Atlantic Sea as you enjoy the locale's freshest gets.

Investigate ocean-side eateries in Albufeira, Lagos, or Olhão, where barbecued sardines, octopus servings of mixed greens, and garlic-implanted prawns entice your taste buds. Jump into the Algarvian custom of "cataplana," a rich fish stew cooked in a unique copper pot. Whether partaking in a feast with a perspective on the sea or relishing the catch of the day in a beguiling fishing town, the fish enjoyments of the Algarve guarantee a gastronomic encounter that mirrors the locale's sea legacy.

Chapter:4

Sintra

Step into the realm of enchantment as we explore Sintra, a fairytale destination where romantic palaces and lush gardens unfold against the backdrop of the Sintra Mountains. In this chapter, wander through the UNESCO-listed historic centre, where pastel-coloured buildings and charming boutiques create a whimsical atmosphere.

Visit the iconic Pena Palace, perched atop the Sintra Hills with its vibrant colours and eclectic architectural styles. Explore the mysterious Initiation Well at Quinta da Regaleira, revealing esoteric symbolism amid captivating gardens. Lose yourself in the narrow streets of the Old Town, where traditional Portuguese tiles and artisan shops beckon.

Sintra, with its magical ambiance and architectural wonders, invites you to delve into a world where fantasy and reality seamlessly converge. Join us on this journey through Sinatra's captivating landscapes and discover why this destination has long been a source of inspiration for poets and dreamers alike.

Enchanting Palaces and Gardens

Captivating Royal Residences and Gardens

Drench yourself in the supernatural universe of Sintra as we investigate its captivating royal residences and nurseries. In this part, find the structural wonders that beauty the Sintra Slopes and the lavish vegetation that encompasses them.

Wonder about the heartfelt Pena Royal residence, a kaleidoscope of varieties roosted on a slope, offering all-encompassing perspectives on the encompassing scene. Walk around the manicured nurseries of Monserrate Royal residence, where fascinating plants and water highlights make a peaceful desert spring. Reveal the persona of Quinta da Regaleira, with its mysterious entries, underground passages, and the entrancing Inception Well.

Sintra's royal residences and nurseries are a demonstration of the imagination of the people who formed this scene. Go along with us on an excursion through these fanciful settings, where each corner recounts an account of sovereignty, dream, and the immortal charm of this enthralling objective.

Pena Palace

Roosted magnificently on the Sintra Slopes, Pena Castle remains an image of sentimentalism and compositional quality. In this part, dive into the fantasy universe of Pena Royal residence, a UNESCO World Legacy site that catches the creative mind.

Investigate the dynamic mix of styles that decorate the royal residence, from Moorish and Gothic impacts to Manueline and Renaissance components. Meander through the extravagant chambers loaded up with period furniture, multifaceted tilework, and luxurious subtleties. Respect the all-encompassing perspectives on the encompassing scene from the castle patios, where the Atlantic Sea and Sintra's lavish woods make a stunning background.

Pena Royal residence welcomes you to step into an existence where dream and reality interweave, offering a brief look into the imagination of nineteenth-century Sentimentalism. Go along with us as we investigate the charming lobbies and gardens of Pena Castle, a building diamond settled in the core of Sintra.

Quinta da Regaleira

Set out on an excursion through the otherworldly grounds of Quinta da Regaleira, a spellbinding home that mixes compositional marvels with obscure imagery. In this part, disentangle the mysteries concealed inside its charming nurseries and lavish designs.

Investigate the famous Commencement Well, an underground pinnacle enhanced with winding flights of stairs and emblematic carvings, reflecting mysterious and catalytic topics. Meander through the rich nurseries, finding stowed-away grottoes, lakes, and the Regaleira House of Prayer. Respect the mixed design of the castle, combining Neo-Manueline, Renaissance, and Gothic styles.

Quinta da Regaleira entices those with a propensity for secret and interest. Go along with us as we dive into the recondite imagery and amazing magnificence that characterise this remarkable domain, welcoming guests to open its deeper implications and drench themselves in its mysterious feeling.

Sinatra's Old Town

Step back in time as we meander through the enchanting paths of Sinatra's Old Town. In this section, submerge yourself in the authentic heart of Sintra, where cobblestone roads wind far beyond customary Portuguese houses embellished with vivid tiles.

Find the genuineness of nearby life as you investigate noteworthy squares like Praça da República, where bistros welcome you to appreciate Portuguese rarities. Walk around slender rear entryways fixed with craftsman shops, offering special artworks and gifts. Visit the Public Castle of Sintra, a middle age fort that has seen hundreds of years of history.

Sinatra's Old Town is an enthralling mix of compositional legacy and neighbourhood fascination, giving a brief look into the rich embroidery of Portugal's past. Go along with us as we wander through these immortal roads, where each corner holds a piece of history and a story to tell.

Chapter: 5

Cultural Gems Across Portugal

Social Diamonds Across Portugal

Set out on a social odyssey as we investigate the different and enhancing social pearls dispersed across Portugal. In this section, find the embroidered artwork of history, expressions, and customs that characterise this charming country.

Fado Music in Coimbra: Submerge yourself in the spirit of blending tunes of Fado, Portugal's conventional music. In Coimbra, the eerie tunes resound through noteworthy roads and catch the embodiment of Portuguese Saudade.

Historical Évora: Excursion to Évora, a UNESCO World Legacy city, where Roman remains, middle-aged roads, and the notorious Sanctuary of Diana weaves a story of Portugal's past.

Maritime Legacy in Aveiro: Investigate the enchanting channels and Workmanship Nouveau design of Aveiro, known as the "Venice of Portugal." Dive into its oceanic history, where vivid Moliceiro boats tell stories of the ocean.

Go along with us as we uncover these social diamonds, each contributing a one-of-a-kind feature to the dynamic mosaic that is Portugal's rich social legacy.

Fado Music in Coimbra

Experience the impactful types of Fado music in the notable city of Coimbra. In this section, dive into the heartfelt tunes that reverberate through the restricted roads and old yards, making an environment of melancholic magnificence.

Visit the College of Coimbra, where the eerie tunes of Fado reverberate in understudy social affairs and neighbourhood Fado houses. Investigate the melodious articulations of yearning and sentimentality that characterise Coimbra Fado, a particular style with male voices and subjects frequently based on college and lost love.

Coimbra's Fado is more than music; it is a social excursion into the feelings and customs that shape the city's personality. Go along with us as we drench ourselves in the enrapturing universe of Coimbra Fado, where each note conveys the heaviness of history and opinion.

Historical Évora

Step into the revered hug of Évora, a city where history murmurs through old walls and cobblestone roads. In this part, investigate the socially woven artwork that acquired Évora its UNESCO World Legacy status.

Visit the very much-saved Roman Sanctuary of Évora, a famous demonstration of the city's Roman past. Walk around Praça do Giraldo, a vivacious square encircled by middle-aged structures and home to the Gothic Évora Church building. Investigate the hauntingly delightful House of Prayer of Bones (Capela dos Ossos), where human bones are coordinated into the design, provoking reflection on the brevity of life.

Évora welcomes you to meander through its environmental back streets, where each step divulges layers of history. Go along with us as we uncover the verifiable fortunes that make Évora an enrapturing objective for those looking for a certified association with Portugal's past.

Maritime Heritage in Aveiro

Sea Legacy in Aveiro

Set out on an oceanic excursion through the trenches of Aveiro, a city where marine practices and Craftsmanship Nouveau polish join. In this part, investigate the special mix of oceanic legacy and structural excellence that characterises this beachfront jewel.

Find the pleasant Moliceiro boats, embellished with dynamic tones and mind-boggling subtleties, as they explore the serene waterways. These boats, once utilised for collecting kelp, presently offer beautiful travels that give a brief look into Aveiro's oceanic history.

Wonder about the Craftsmanship Nouveau veneers along the trenches, displaying the city's engineering extravagance. Visit the Sea Historical Center of Ílhavo to dig further into Aveiro's nautical past, where displays describe stories of fishing, shipbuilding, and the district's association with the ocean.

Go along with us as we explore the waters of Aveiro, where oceanic legacy and social appeal make an extraordinary scene along the sun-doused Portuguese coast.

Chapter:6

Gastronomic Adventures

Set out on a culinary odyssey through Portugal's different and luscious gastronomic scene. In this section, enjoy the flavours that characterise the country's rich culinary legacy, from conventional dishes to contemporary joys.

Culinary Delights: Enjoy the fragrant marvels of Portuguese cooking, from the notable Bacalhau (salted cod) to generous stews like Feijoada. Investigate territorial strengths that grandstand the assorted impacts of Portugal's set of experiences and topography.

Wine Tasting Experiences: Adventure into the grape plantations of the Douro Valley or the Alentejo district, where Portugal's prestigious wines become fully awake. Appreciate tastings of Port wine, Vinho Verde, and the rich reds that describe Portuguese viticulture.

Local Markets and Flavors: Submerge yourself in the dynamic air of nearby business sectors, similar to Lisbon's Mercado da Ribeira or Porto's Mercado do Bolhão. Test distinctive cheeses, relieved meats, and new produce that mirror the validity of Portuguese gastronomy.

Go along with us as we investigate the different and scrumptious universe of Portuguese cooking, where each dish recounts a story and each chomp is a festival of the country's culinary imaginativeness.

Culinary Delights

Leave on a tangible excursion through the different and flavorful universe of Portuguese culinary joys. In this part, appreciate the rich embroidered artwork of flavours that portray the country's gastronomic legacy.

Bacalhau (Salted Cod): Investigate the heap ways Bacalhau is ready, from Bacalhau à Brás to Bacalhau com Natas. This notorious dish mirrors Portugal's verifiable association with the ocean.

Caldo Verde: Savour the experience of the effortlessness and goodness of Caldo Verde, a consoling green soup made with kale, potatoes, and chorizo.

Pastel de Nata: Enjoy the sweet flawlessness of Pastel de Nata, a custard tart with a fresh baked good shell, frequently delighted in with a sprinkle of cinnamon.

Francesinha: Experience the intense kinds of Francesinha, a generous sandwich beginning from Porto, highlighting relieved meats, linguiça, and a fiery sauce.

From new fish to generous stews, each dish tells a story of Portugal's culinary practices. Go along with us as we explore the culinary joys that make feasting in Portugal a delightful and remarkable experience.

Wine Tasting Experiences

Set out on a brilliant excursion through Portugal's grape plantations and relish the extravagance of its wine culture. In this part, we investigate the assorted scenes that produce a portion of the world's best wines.

Douro Valley Vineyards: Navigate the terraced slopes of the Douro Valley, a UNESCO World Legacy site, and enjoy wine samplings in the beautiful magnificence of Portugal's head wine district.

Port Wine Basements in Porto: Slide into the notable wine basements of Vila Nova de Gaia, confronting Porto across the Douro Stream. Here is an example of the sweet intricacies of Port wine, and find out about the specialty of its creation.

Alentejo's Rich Reds: Dare to the Alentejo district, known for its huge fields and strong red wines. Investigate family-claimed grape plantations and appreciate tastings of hearty reds that mirror the warm environment and one-of-a-kind terroir.

Vinho Verde Adventures: Experience the fizz of Vinho Verde in the rich green scenes of the Minho area. Find fresh and invigorating wines that impeccably supplement Portugal's fish food.

Go along with us as we open up the insider facts of Portugal's grape plantations, where each glass recounts an account of custom, development, and the terroir that shapes the personality of Portuguese wines. Cheers to a wine-sampling venture that waits on the sense of taste and in the heart.

Local Markets and Flavours

Nearby Business sectors and Flavours

Submerge yourself in the energetic embroidery of Portugal's culinary scene by investigating its exuberant nearby business sectors. In this part, meander through clamouring commercial centres where the air is loaded up with the fragrances of new produce, flavours, and high-quality joys.

Mercado da Ribeira in Lisbon: Plunge into the tangible joy of Lisbon's Mercado da Ribeira, where slows down burst with vivid organic products, vegetables, and a variety of conventional Portuguese items. Test nearby cheeses, restored meats, and newly got fish.

Mercado do Bolhão in Porto: Investigate the noteworthy Mercado do Bolhão in Porto, a clamouring market where merchants offer a kaleidoscope of new natural products, vegetables, and provincial fortes. Draw in with neighbourhood merchants to find the tales behind their items.

Aveiro's Fish Market: Visit the fish market in Aveiro, where the day's catch shows up straight from the ocean. Drench yourself in the sea climate as you witness the dynamic presentation of fish that graces the market slows down.

Olhão's Metropolitan Market: Experience the credibility of Olhão's Civil Market in the Algarve, where fishmongers, ranchers, and craftsmen unite to feature the area's assorted flavours. From olives and almonds to figs and territorial wines, the market is a gold mine of Algarvian strengths.

Go along with us as we explore these vivacious business sectors, where the beat of Portuguese culinary practices beats intensely. Test, investigate, and take pleasure in the wealth of nearby flavours that make these business sectors a fundamental piece of the Portuguese gastronomic experience.

Chapter: 7

Outdoor Escapes

OpOpen-airscapes

Leave on an experience in Portugal's normal miracles and open-air scenes. In this part, we investigate the different and amazing conditions that coax open-arians and nature sweethearts.

Douro Valley Vineyards: Cross the terraced grape plantations of the Douro Valley, a UNESCO World Legacy site, where the shocking scenes are essentially as inebriating as the wines. Climb or bicycle through the slopes, enjoying all-encompassing perspectives on the wandering Douro Stream.

Hiking in Peneda-Gerês Public Park: Trim up your climbing boots for an investigation of Peneda-Gerês Public Park, Portugal's only public park. Find lavish woods, flowing cascades, and uneven landscape, giving a safe house to widely varied vegetation.

Adventure in the Azores: Leave on an outside caper in the Azores, an archipelago in the Atlantic Sea. Investigate volcanic scenes, climb along beachfront precipices, and enjoy water exercises, for example, whale watching and plunging.

Whether you look for the serenity of grape plantation vistas, the rough excellence of public parks, or the untamed charm of island scenes, Portugal offers open-air gets away from that commitment experience, unwinding, and a significant association with nature.

Douro Valley Vineyards

Welcome to the stunning Douro Valley, where the creativity of winemaking unfurls amid terraced grape plantations and wandering riverbanks. In this section, we dive into the captivating scenes and wine customs that have procured the Douro Valley its UNESCO World Legacy status.

Terraced Splendour: Observe the hypnotising terraced slopes, carefully cut to support grape plantations that stretch as may be obvious. The patios exhibit the creativity of viticulture as well as deal with an all-encompassing material that develops with the evolving light.

Wine Domains and Quintas: Investigate recognized wine homes and quintas, each with its extraordinary appeal and winemaking theory. Participate in tastings of widely acclaimed Ports, vigorous reds, and fragrant whites, all while encompassed by the quietness of the valley.

Scenic Cruises: Improve your Douro Valley experience with a relaxed voyage along the Douro Waterway. Float between the terraced slants, acquiring an alternate point of view of the plant-covered slopes and memorable wine homes.

Cultural Heritage: Submerge yourself in the social embroidered artwork of winemaking families who have tended these plants for ages. Find the well-established methods and present-day developments that blend to create the remarkable wines inseparable from the Douro Valley.

As we investigate the Douro Valley grape plantations, go along with us in raising a glass to the agreeable mix of nature, legacy, and craftsmanship that characterises this exceptional wine locale in Portugal.

Hiking in Peneda-Gerês National Park

Climbing in Peneda-Gerês Public Park

Leave on an excursion through the untamed magnificence of Peneda-Gerês Public Park, Portugal's just public park. In this part, we ribbon up our climbing boots to investigate the different scenes, from rich backwoods to rough mountains, that make this park a safe house for outside lovers.

Trailblazing Adventures: Find a broad organisation of climbing trails that jumble the recreation area, offering courses for all degrees of explorers. Navigate antiquated Roman streets, climb stone pinnacles, and wander through tranquil valleys, all while drenching yourself in the immaculate wild.

Waterfall Wonders: Experience the recreation area's various cascades, like the famous Tahiti Cascade. Revive yourself in the cool mountain streams and relish the peacefulness of these regular marvels concealed in the core of the recreation area.

Wildlife Encounters: Peneda-Gerês is home to different verdures. Watch out for wild Garrano ponies, Iberian wolves, and the tricky brilliant hawk as you adventure further into the recreation area. The biodiversity here makes an enamoring scenery for your climbing ventures.

Historical Mysteries: Investigate the recreation area's verifiable destinations, including old stone storehouses and customary mountain towns. Reveal the rich social legacy that has moulded the existences of the individuals who have called these scenes home for a long time.

Go along with us as we explore the paths of Peneda-Gerês Public Park, where each step uncovers another feature of nature's quality and social history. Whether you look for testing risings or relaxed walks, the recreation area welcomes you to encounter the crude magnificence of Portugal's open-air scenes.

Adventure in the Azores

Undertakings in the Azores

Leave on a thrilling excursion through the Azores, an archipelago of volcanic islands in the Atlantic Sea. In this part, we jump into the different open-air undertakings that anticipate those looking for adrenaline-syphoning encounters amid dazzling scenes.

Whale Watching: Set forth on the Atlantic waters for a completely exhilarating whale-watching experience. Experience grand cetaceans, for example, sperm whales, dolphins, and blue whales right at home, making a marine scene remarkable to the Azores.

Volcanic Exploration: Investigate the volcanic scenes that characterise the Azores. Climb to the culmination of Mount Pico, the most noteworthy top in Portugal, or navigate the volcanic holes of Sete Cidades, where emerald-green and blue lakes contrast against the dark soil.

Hot Springs and Warm Baths: Unwind and revive in the normal underground aquifers dissipated across the islands. Partake in a calming dunk in the warm waters of the Furnace geothermal springs or loosen up in the one-of-a-kind warm pools of Land Nostra Nursery in São Miguel.

Scuba Jumping and Snorkelling: Plunge into the clear waters encompassing the Azores for a submerged experience. Investigate lively coral reefs, and submerged caverns, and experience assorted marine life, from beautiful fish to elegant manta beams.

The Azores offer a jungle gym for outside lovers, where the excitement of experience meets the immaculate excellence of nature. Go along with us as we uncover the different and energising exercises that make the Azores a remarkable objective for those looking for extraordinary capers.

P☐☐O ☐☐T☐☐U☐☐G☐☐A☐☐L

Chapter:8

Festivals and Celebrations

Submerge yourself in the dynamic embroidered artwork of Portuguese culture by investigating its exuberant celebrations and festivities. In this section, we dig into the lively occasions that exhibit the country's rich practices, music, and local area soul.

Lisbon's Santo António Festival: Join the energetic festivals of Lisbon's benefactor holy person, Santo António. Experience the beautiful motorcades, enthusiastic road parties, and conventional weddings that fill the city's memorable neighbourhoods with bliss and energy.

Carnival in Torres Vedras: Revel in the abundance of Amusement parkin Torres Vedras, famous for its exuberant motorcades, energetic ensembles, and humorous floats. Join local people in this energetic festival that consolidates custom with contemporary energy.

Fado Evenings in Coimbra: Submerge yourself in the frightful tunes of Fado during the yearly Festa de Santo António in Coimbra. Experience outdoor shows, customary parades, and the spirit blending hints of Portugal's famous music.

Madeira Blossom Festival: Witness the island of Madeira burst into a mob of varieties during the Bloom Celebration. Wonder about botanical floats, marches, and complicated blossom covers that decorate the roads, making a stunning scene.

Porto Wine Fest: Raise a glass to Porto's wine legacy during the Porto Wine Fest. Appreciate tastings, wine pairings, and widespread developments set against the scenery of the Douro Waterway, commending the city's getting through association with its well-known.

Go along with us as we participate in these happy minutes, where the glow of Portuguese cordiality meets with the delight of festivity, making recollections that wait long after the celebrations have finished.

Carnaval

Carnaval in Portugal

Prepare to release your merry soul as we dig into the lively festival of Carnival in Portugal. In this part, experience the brilliant and vigorous celebration that denotes this cheerful event.

Torres Vedras Carnival: Join the energetic Amusement park festivities in Torres Vedras, known for its extravagant processions, elaborate outfits, and humorous floats. This lively occasion grandstands the local area's inventiveness and humour, making it a must-visit objective during the Fair season.

Loule Festival in Algarve: Drench yourself in the exuberant air of Loule Fair in the Algarve. Witness beautiful parades including themed floats, customary music, and enthusiastic dance exhibitions that dazzle local people and guests the same.

Over Carnival: Investigate the dynamic Ovar Amusement Park, celebrated with terrific motorcades, enthusiastic music, and elaborate ensembles. This customary Amusement park is prestigious for its noteworthy presentations and the excited cooperation of the neighbourhood local area.

Madeira Carnival: Experience the Festival wizardry on the island of Madeira, where lively processions wind through the roads embellished with beautiful outfits and amazing enrichments. Revel in the bubbly climate and partake in the exuberant amusement that describes Madeira's Fair.

As we step into the universe of Carnaval in Portugal, prepare to be cleared away by the mood, variety, and richness that characterise this upbeat festival. From North to South, Portugal's Carnaval is a dining experience for the faculties, welcoming everybody to participate in the energetic celebrations.

Fado Festivals

Fado Celebrations in Portugal

Submerge yourself in the spirit-blending tunes of Fado as we investigate the captivating universe of Fado celebrations in Portugal. In this section, find the occasions that observe Portugal's notorious music, uniting energetic entertainers and aficionados.

Festival de Fado de Alfama, Lisbon: Excursion to the notable Alfama locale in Lisbon during the Celebration de Fado de Alfama. Experience the thin roads and private settings loaded up with the frightful hints of Fado, as neighbourhood and global craftsmen meet up to commend this treasured melodic custom.

Amália Rodrigues Fado Celebration, Lisbon:
Give proper respect to the "Sovereign of Fado" at the Amália Rodrigues Fado Celebration in Lisbon. Named after the incredible Fado vocalist, this celebration praises her inheritance with exhibitions by contemporary Fado specialists who keep on dazzling crowds with their emotive voices.

Caixa Alfama, Lisbon: Investigate the Caixa Alfama Fado Celebration, a yearly occasion that changes the Alfama region into a phase for Fado exhibitions. Meander through the pleasant rear entryways and squares to find a different setup of Fado specialists, exhibiting the class' close-to-home profundity and social importance.

Festival Internacional de Fado de Cascais: Experience the Worldwide Fado Celebration in Cascais, where the ocean-side feeling upgrades the profound reverberation of Fado. This celebration draws in both prepared Fado devotees and novices, making a unique environment of appreciation and festivity.

Go along with us as we embrace the energy and despairing of Fado at these celebrations, where the music winds around a story of affection, yearning, and the significant pith of Portuguese culture.

Traditional Saints' Days

Conventional Holy People's Days in Portugal

Plunge into the rich woven artwork of Portuguese practices by investigating the festivals of conventional holy people's days. In this section, find the social and strict merriments that honour holy people across various areas of Portugal.

Santo António (Holy person Anthony) - Lisbon: Experience the energetic festivals of Santo António in Lisbon, the city's benefactor holy person. Witness energetic parades, road parties, and the customary "Weddings of Santo António," where couples from varying backgrounds partake in mock weddings.

São João (Holy person John) - Porto: Join the energetic São João festivities in Porto, where the roads wake up with music, dance, and the trading of sweet-smelling spices known as "mavericks." The feature of the night is the fabulous light show over the Douro Stream.

São Pedro (Holy person Peter) - Póvoa de Varzim: Investigate the sea customs of São Pedro in Póvoa de Varzim, a waterfront town. Witness the energetic parades of anglers and boats enhanced with blossoms, respecting São Pedro, the benefactor holy person of anglers.

Senhor Santo Cristo dos Milagres - Ponta Delgada, Azores: Submerge yourself in the strict enthusiasm of Senhor Santo Cristo dos Milagres in Ponta Delgada, Azores. This strict parade and celebration draw a huge number of pioneers, making a strong articulation of confidence.

Experience the enchantment of these customary holy people's days, where strict commitment interlaces with social merriments, making an extraordinary mix of otherworldliness and local area festivity across Portugal.

Chapter: 9

Practicalities

Reasonable items for Going to Portugal

In this part, we dive into the reasonable parts of going to Portugal, offering bits of knowledge and tips to guarantee a smooth and pleasant excursion.

Transportation: Investigate the proficient and various transportation choices, including trains, transports, and the broad organisation of interstates. Explore the beguiling urban areas effortlessly and find the beautiful field utilising Portugal's all-around associated transportation framework.

Accommodations: Explore the range of facilities, from notable pousadas to current lodgings and beguiling guesthouses. Track down the ideal spot to remain that suits your inclinations and improves your general travel insight.

Cuisine and Feasting Etiquette: Jump into the culinary scene with tips on conventional dishes, famous restaurants, and eating manners. Find the subtleties of Portuguese cooking and enjoy nearby strengths in a socially conscious way.

Language and Communication: Look into fundamental Portuguese expressions and customs to upgrade your cooperation with local people. Embrace the glow of Portuguese cordiality by embracing the neighbourhood language.

Currency and Finances: Grasp the money, banking offices, and instalment techniques predominant in Portugal. Guarantee smooth monetary exchanges and planning during your movements.

Weather and Packing: Plan for changing environments by grasping Portugal's atmospheric conditions. Pack likewise to guarantee solace and readiness for the assorted scenes you'll experience.

Safety and Health: Focus on security with data on crisis administrations, wellbeing offices, and travel protection. Remain informed about nearby traditions to guarantee a conscious and secure travel insight.

Go along with us as we explore the items of common sense of going to Portugal, furnishing you with the fundamental apparatuses to take full advantage of your excursion and make enduring recollections in this enamoring objective.

Transportation Tips

Transportation Ways to Go in Portugal

Explore Portugal's different scenes easily utilising these transportation tips:

Trains: Appreciate beautiful train ventures associated with significant urban communities. Buy tickets ahead of time for famous courses, and consider rail passes for adaptability.

Buses: Investigate urban communities and towns effectively using Portugal's broad transport organisation. Provincial and intercity transport gives a practical method for movement.

Car Rentals: Think about leasing a vehicle to investigate distant regions. Know about tolls on thruways, and embrace the opportunity of driving along beautiful courses.

Metro and Trams: In urban areas like Lisbon and Porto, use metro frameworks and famous cable cars for advantageous metropolitan travel. Buy battery-powered metro cards for practical rides.

Taxis and Ride-sharing: Cabs are promptly accessible, and ride-sharing administrations work in significant urban communities. Affirm tolls ahead of time, and utilise trustworthy administrations for security.

Walking and Cycling: Find the appeal of urban areas by walking, particularly in noteworthy locales. Lease bikes for a relaxed investigation of picturesque regions and seaside ways.

Ferries and Boats: Experience beachfront urban areas and islands with ship administrations. Appreciate boat trips along waterways or to seaward objections for a novel viewpoint.

Timeliness: Know about plans for trains, transports, and other transportation modes. Reliability is for the most part expected, so plan in a like manner.

Language Barrier: English is broadly spoken, however learning fundamental Portuguese expressions can improve collaborations, particularly in additional ar-off regions.

Parking: Assuming that driving, be aware of stopping guidelines. In urban areas, choose secure leaving offices to guarantee the well-being of your vehicle.

By integrating these transportation tips into your itinerary items, you'll explore Portugal consistently, opening the country's different scenes and social fortunes.

Language and Etiquette

Language and Manners in Portugal

Improve your movement experience by grasping the language and decorum subtleties in Portugal:

Language

Portuguese Phrases: While numerous local people communicate in English, learning fundamental Portuguese expressions, for example, good tidings and typical statements is valued and encourages a positive association.

Pronunciation: Portuguese has explicit sounds, so practise elocutions to effectively be seen more.

Greeting Etiquette

Handshakes and Kisses: A handshake is normal for good tidings, while dear loved ones might trade kisses on the two cheeks. Follow the lead of local people.

Dining Etiquette

Politeness: Stand by to be situated in eateries, and utilise considerate expressions like "Por favour" (please) and "Obrigado/a" (much obliged).

Tipping: An administration charge is frequently included, however, it is standard to leave a little tip.

Cultural Respect

Regarding Elders: Recognize more established people, utilising titles like "Senhor" or "Senhora."

Moderate Dress: In additional customary regions, unassuming attire is valued, particularly while visiting holy places or strict locales.

Personal Space

Actual Contact: Portuguese individuals are by and large amicable, however, be aware of individual space. Keep away from inordinate actual contact with colleagues.

Time Management

Punctuality: Show up on time for arrangements and parties. While the speed might be loose, reliability is esteemed.

Expressing Gratitude

Graciousness: Express appreciation for cordiality, feasts, or help with authentic appreciation. "Muito /a" signifies "Much thanks."

Cultural Sensitivity

Strict Customs: Regard strict practices and practices, particularly while visiting chapels or partaking in neighbourhood occasions.

By embracing the language and decorum, you'll cultivate positive associations with local people, improve your social experience, and explore social circumstances with effortlessness during your time in Portugal.

Safety Considerations

Security Contemplations for Going to Portugal

Guarantee a protected and charming excursion by remembering these well-being contemplations during your visit to Portugal

Emergency Contacts

Realise the nearby crisis numbers: 112 for general crises, and 115 for woodland fires.

Health Precautions

- Convey important meds and a fundamental emergency treatment pack.

- Remain hydrated, particularly during hotter months.

- Find out more about the area of clinical offices.

Criminal Awareness

- Practice sound judgement in jam-packed regions to forestall pickpocketing.
- Keep resources secure and be careful in traveller-weighty areas.

Traffic Safety

- Notice traffic rules while going across roads.
- Be careful while driving, particularly in new regions.

Natural Hazards

- Focus on climate alerts, particularly during the stormy season.
- Observe security rules if partaking in outside exercises.

Coastal Safety

- Stick to cautioning signs on sea shores and adhere to lifeguard guidelines.
- Be mindful of solid flows and waves.

Local Customs

- Regard neighbourhood customs and social awareness.

- Follow decorum in strict destinations and during conventional occasions.

Language Barrier

- Save a fundamental comprehension of Portuguese expressions for correspondence.

COVID-19 Guidelines

- Remain informed about current Coronavirus rules and limitations.

- Follow well-being conventions, including cover-wearing and social separating.

Travel Insurance

- Get extensive travel protection covering wellbeing crises and other unanticipated circumstances.

By remaining informed and practising alert, you can add to a protected and pleasant involvement with Portugal. Find out about nearby traditions, adhere to safe and secure rules, and stay watchful to capitalise on your movements.

Conclusion

As your investigation of Portugal unfurls, may the dynamic scenes, rich social embroidered artwork, and warm neighbourliness wait in your recollections. From the noteworthy roads of Lisbon to the terraced grape plantations of the Douro Valley, Portugal offers an enthralling excursion through time and custom.

As you enjoy the kinds of Portuguese cooking, submerge yourself in the heartfelt tunes of Fado, and embrace the energetic festivals, recollect that each step uncovers a story. Whether meandering through Alfama or climbing in Peneda-Gerês, each experience adds to the mosaic of your Portuguese experience.

Portugal, with its mix of history, nature, and social wealth, welcomes you to enjoy the experiences, interface with local people, and relish the enchantment of this enthralling objective. Whether you look for the serenity of the Algarve's immaculate sea shores or the energy of Lisbon's dynamic roads, Portugal guarantees an extraordinary excursion.

As you bid goodbye to this captivating area, may the recollections wait, and the soul of Portugal stay with you, repeating the reverberations of Fado, the murmurs of history, and the glow of its kin. Until we meet again on your next investigation, may your movements be loaded up with disclosure, euphoria, and a feeling of association with the different miracles of our reality. Safe voyages and Adeus!

Reflecting on Your Portuguese

Pondering the Portugal travel guide, it's clear that Portugal is a nation of different magnificence, rich history, and dynamic culture. From the beautiful roads of Lisbon to the sun-kissed seashores of the Algarve, each corner offers an exceptional and captivating experience.

The investigation of Portugal unwound the mind-boggling mix of conventional and present-day impacts, displayed in its engineering, cooking, and celebrations. The parts on Fado celebrations, customary holy people's days, and the different scenes of the Douro Valley and Peneda-Gerês Public Park give a brief look into the social and regular ponders that anticipate explorers.

Language and behaviour tips underscore the significance of interfacing with local people, while well-being contemplations guarantee a protected and charming excursion. Reasonable items like transportation, facilities, and culinary joys act as significant aides for those wanting to investigate this dazzling objective.

All in all, Portugal remains as an embroidery of encounters, where the glow of its kind, the reverberations of Fado, and the immortal excellence of its scenes meet. Whether you're a set of experiences devotee, a culinary traveller, or a nature sweetheart, Portugal welcomes you to leave on an excursion loaded up with revelations, making recollections that get through lengthy after the experience closes. Adeus to Portugal, a land that entices with great enthusiasm those looking for an embroidery of social lavishness and normal wonder.

Adventure

Set out on experiences in Portugal, where each step uncovers a universe of conceivable outcomes

Douro Valley Exploration: Navigate the terraced grape plantations of the Douro Valley, relishing the kinds of eminent wines and cruising along the winding stream.

Hiking in Peneda-Gerês Public Park: Ribbon up your boots to investigate rich woods, flowing cascades, and rough mountains in Portugal's just public park.

Azorean Escapades: Plunge into the Azores, a domain of volcanic scenes and marine miracles. From whale watching to climbing holes, each second is an undertaking.

Cultural Submersion in Lisbon and Porto: Meander through notable regions, find famous tourist spots, and embrace the dynamic social scenes of Lisbon and Porto.

Fado Festivals: Submerge yourself in the eerie songs of Fado at celebrations in Alfama, Lisbon, and other charming settings across Portugal.

Beach Rapture in the Algarve: Loll in the sun on the Algarve's perfect sea shores, investigating stowed away bays and enjoying fish delights.

Historical Journeys in Sintra: Reveal the captivating royal residences and nurseries of Sintra, a UNESCO World Legacy site that transports you to a fantasy domain.

Whether you're attracted to the social heartbeat of urban communities, the untamed magnificence of nature, or the heartfelt tunes of Fado, Portugal offers an embroidery of experiences ready to be investigated. Allow each experience to shape a section of your process in this enrapturing objective.

Appendix

Surely! Here is an example structure for a reference section in the Portugal travel guide:

Index: Valuable Assets and Extra Information

Travel Applications and Websites: Suggestions for movement arranging, language interpretation, and route applications/sites.

Detailed Maps: Top-notch guides of significant urban communities, locales, and well-known traveller objections.

Culinary Glossary: A glossary of fundamental Portuguese culinary terms for requesting at cafés or investigating nearby business sectors.

Useful Contacts: Crisis contact numbers, neighbourhood specialists, and consulate data.

Packing Checklist: An agenda to guarantee you have every one of the basics for your outing to Portugal.

Further Reading: Book proposals for those keen on diving further into Portuguese history, culture, and cooking.

Language Phrasebook: A drawn-out rundown of supportive Portuguese expressions for different circumstances.

Transportation Timetables: Connections or subtleties on train, transport, and ship schedules for reference during movement.

Currency Conversion: Tips on cash trade and a transformation diagram for normal costs.

Safety Guidelines: Point-by-point wellbeing rules, crisis strategies, and wellbeing suggestions.

Customs and Behavior Summary: A succinct outline of social standards and decorum to improve social comprehension.

Acknowledgments: A part recognizing sources, patrons, or associations that gave significant bits of knowledge during the formation of the movement guide.

Go ahead and redo this construction given the particular substance and data you need to remember for the reference section of your Portugal travel guide.

Useful Phrases in Portuguese

Positively! Here are some helpful expressions in Portuguese to improve your correspondence during your movements in Portugal:

Greetings:
- Hi - Olá
- Hello - Bom dia
- Good evening - Boa tarde
- Goodbye - Boa noite

Politeness:

- Please - Por favour

- Much obliged to you - Obrigado (for guys)/Obrigada (for females)

- Excuse me - Com licença/Desculpe

Common Expressions:

- Indeed - Sim

- No - Não

- Excuse me/Exculpation - Desculpe

- Please accept my apologies - Desculpe/Peço desculpa

Basic Conversational Phrases:

- How are you? - Como está?

- I'm fine, thank you - Estou bem, obrigado/a

- What is your name? - Como se chama?

- My name is... - Chamo-me...

Directions:

- Where is...? - Onde fica...?

- Right - À direita

- Left - À esquerda

- Straight ahead - Em frente

Eating and Drinking:

- Menu, please - O menu, favour
- I would like... - Gostaria de...
- Water - Água
- The check, please - A, favour

Numbers:

- 1 - Um
- 2 - Dois
- 3 - Três
- 10 - Dez

Time:

- What time is it? - Que horas são?
- It's [time] - São [hora]

Shopping:

- What amount does this cost? - Quanto isto?
- Might I at any point pay with a card? - Posso pagar com cartão?

Emergencies:

  - Help! - Socorro!

  - I want a specialist - Preciso de um médico

  - Where is the closest emergency clinic? - Onde fica o medical clinic mais próximo?

Go ahead and practise these expressions to make your connections smoother during your visit to Portugal. Boa Viagem (Safe voyages)!

Recommended Reading and Resources

Suggested Readings and Assets for Investigating Portugal:

Books:

  - "The Book of Uneasiness" by Fernando Pessoa

  - A philosophical work catching the pith of Lisbon through the eyes of its confounding writer.

  -" A Little Passing in Lisbon" by Robert Wilson

- A grasping secret novel that winds around together verifiable occasions and current wrongdoing in Lisbon.

Travel Guides:

- Desolate Planet Portugal
- A far-reaching guide covering different parts of Portugal, from notable urban communities to beachfront pearls.
- Rick Steves Portugal
- Offers useful guidance and social experiences for voyagers investigating Portugal.

Culinary Exploration:

- "Portuguese Homestyle Cooking" by Ana Patuleia Ortins
- An investigation of conventional Portuguese recipes and cooking methods.
- "The Food of Portugal" by Jean Anderson
- A culinary excursion through Portugal, highlighting bona fide recipes and provincial strengths.

Historical and Social Insights:

- "The Historical backdrop of Portugal" by Paulo Jorge de Sousa Pinto
- An available outline of Portugal's intricate history.
- "Portugal: A Buddy History" by José H. Saraiva
- Investigates Portugal's set of experiences from ancient times to the present.

Language Learning:

- Duolingo
- An intuitive application for learning Portuguese, offering functional language abilities for explorers.
- BBC Dialects - Portuguese
- Online language illustrations with sound and video assets.

Online Resources:

- Visit Portugal
- The authority of the travel industry site gives important data on objections, occasions, and travel tips.
- Culture Outing - Portugal
- Articles covering different parts of Portuguese culture, food, and travel.

Film and Documentaries:

- "Unthinkable" (2012)

- An outwardly dazzling film set in both contemporary and pilgrim period Portugal.

- "Portugal: A Story of Two Urban Communities" (BBC Documentary)

- Investigates the differences between Lisbon and Porto.

Podcasts:

- Portuguese With Carla

- A digital broadcast offering language illustrations and social bits of knowledge.

- Rick Steves' Sound Europe

- Portugal

- Sound aides giving travel tips and social settings.

These assets offer a different scope of viewpoints to improve your comprehension and enthusiasm for Portugal. Whether you're keen on history, food, or language, these suggestions give significant bits of knowledge to your investigation.

Index

Surely! Here is a continuation and finish of the End and List for your Portugal travel guide:

Conclusion:

As you ponder your excursion through the pages of this aide, may the soul of Portugal wait — an embroidery woven with the reverberations of Fado, the glow of its kin, and the immortal charm of its scenes. Portugal coaxes with a novel mix of history, culture, and normal marvels, welcoming explorers to enjoy each experience and make enduring recollections. Adeus to Portugal is an objective that reverberates with appeal, variety, and a charming feeling of disclosure.

Index:

Introduction

Welcoming Portugal

- Social Decorum
- Warmth of Portuguese Neighborliness

City Destinations

- Lisbon
  - Memorable Alfama
  - Present day Energies in Bairro Alto
  - Belem and Its Tourist spots
  - Porto
  - Investigating the Ribeira Area
  - Port Wine Basements Experience
  - Superb Extensions of Porto

Coastal Retreats

- The Algarve
  - Sun-Kissed Shore
  - Immaculate Sea shores
  - Beguiling Waterfront Town
  - Fish Pleasures

Enchanting Sintra

- Captivating Castles and Gardens
- Pena Royal residence
- Quinta da Regaleira

- Sinatra's Old Town

Exploring Portugal

- Fado Music in Coimbra
- Verifiable Évora
- Oceanic Legacy in Aveiro

Culinary Odyssey

- Gastronomic Undertakings
  - Culinary Enjoyments
  - Wine sampling Encounters
  - Neighborhood Markets and Flavours

Outdoor Escapes

- Climbing in Peneda-Gerês Public Park
- Undertakings in the Azores
- Douro Valley Grape plantations

Festivals and Celebrations

- Lisbon's Santo António Celebration
- Amusement park
- Fado Celebrations

Practicalities

Conclusion

Appendix

Recommended Readings and Resources

Index

May this guide act as your sidekick in revealing the miracles of Portugal, directing you through its urban areas, coasts, and social embroidery. Safe ventures and may your experience in Portugal be loaded up with investigation, delight, and extraordinary minutes. Adeus!

Printed in Great Britain
by Amazon

40717976R00066